LOVE & SENSUALITY

Also by Michael R. Lane

Poetry
A Drop of Midnight
Sandbox
Mortal Thoughts
A Leap Year of Haiku

Fiction
Emancipation
UFOs and God
The Family Stone

Mysteries
The Gem Connection
Blue Sun
The Butcher
Six Weeks

LOVE & SENSUALITY

~Poems~

Michael R. Lane

BARE BONES PRESS
P.O. Box 9653, Seattle, WA 98109

Copyright © 2021 Michael R. Lane

ISBN: 978-0-97164-533-2

All rights reserved. No part of this publication may be reproduced, stored in a retrieval system, or transmitted in any form or by any means, electronic, mechanical, recording or otherwise, without the prior written permission of the author.

Published by Bare Bones Press, Seattle, Washington.

Design: Bare Bones Press
Production: Bare Bones Press
Cover Art: Michael R. Lane

Bare Bones Press
P.O. Box 9653
Seattle, WA 98109

www.michaelrlane.com
www.barebonespress.com

Second Edition: August 2023

For the stunning women in my life who nurtured in me the succulent differences between love, passion and sensuality.

May your heart and libido forever be one.

POET'S NOTE

Love & Sensuality are not synonyms no more than marriage and love. While one may be motivated by the other, they can and do exist on separate planes. Love is magnetic, stimulating, powerful and consuming. It is a natural spring for family, dear friends and spouses. Love can be boundless as humanity or refined to our tiny circle of life. There is no right or wrong with love. The heart does not discriminate in that manor. Explaining why a crystal clear destructive relationship to others the one who has fallen remains too blind to see.

Sensuality is seductive, charming, witty, hypnotic and playful. The softer sister of carnal lust. The heart does not have to be in play for sensuality. She enjoys the game and controls the sport. A kiss, a touch, a look or a glance are a few of the gifts she possess to tease your erotic appetite. Words can also join the dance as she weaves her titillating web that may or may not lead to romance.

Sensuality is the lure while love is the hook. One likes to play. The other takes charge. The writings in *Love & Sensuality* explore the sensual and adoration in both its classic and ethereal forms.

Stow your inhibitions for a brief hour or two, relax, savor the music and enjoy the dance.

Contents

Love	1
The I Factor	3
First Meeting	5
Bliss	7
Dawning of a Dream	9
Diamonds	11
Slavery	13
Bound for Home	15
Heaven and Earth	17
Water Love	19
Ra	21
Garden	23
Silver Needle, Silver Hair	25
Brass Button	27
Cradle of Wisdom	29
Parenthood	31
Life Force	33
Heaven's Gate	35
Pleasure	37
Speak Not	39
Bashful	41
Ballads, Lyrics and Melodies (A Love Poem)	43
Her Beauty Makes Me Bashful	45
Alone	47
While Working	49
Rapture	51
Engaged	53
Pleasure	55
Us	57
Soul Mate	59
Woman	61
I Don't Wanna Be No Superman	63
Elegance	65
Probing For Desire	67

True Love Lies	71
Criminal Passion	73
ESP	75
Burn	77
I Won't, I Will	79
So Long, Sweetheart	81
Missing You	83
Stone Heart	85
Distance	87
Estranged	89
Writing, My Love	91
Absence of Desire	93
Paradise	95
Infinite Loves	97
Lonely Heart	99
Self Sacrifice	101
Henna Eyes	103
Human Contact	105
Unexpected Rendezvous	107
Infatuation	109
Potpourri, Kiss Me and Soul	111
Longings	113
Scripture	115
Harmony and Grace	117
Love Eternal	119
Notes	121
Acknowledgements	123

LOVE & SENSUALITY

Love

Funny word love,
four letters
sounds like dove
rhymes with glove
but seldom coos
and rarely fits.

The I Factor

A writer
sparked by the I Factor
scrambles to excite
cinders of possibilities.

Pen groping paper records:
characters
scenes
metaphors
action
similes
dialogue.

Thunder clouds
of reminiscences,
emotions,
moods,
swish violently through
his conscious filter.

Hasty attempts to transcribe
abstract piecemeal
into 3-D reality
disperse
dissolve
spear the heart
of his bright
gray light.

The fever breaks.
The writer is gutted
salvaging minute portions
of random wares
before most
flash to flames.

Blindly his search continues
until another door –
unexpectedly –
swoops open,
granting bantam peeks
at variant futures.

First Meeting

Our eyes touched
fusing two beings,
      one.

Conversation pranced delicately
mind to tongue,
      facilely.

I remember speculating
fascination be this,
      attraction?

Emotional prey
romance ravished souls,
      feasting.

First meeting
encapsulated in heart-light,
      forever.

Bliss

A deep piano voice
with a firm and tender gaze
gives merit to her eyes
engulfed in clover honey glaze,

a spirit ever glowing
in the mirror of her soul
eternally marred, rarely hidden
often shadowed, sometimes dazed,

since none's life is all pleasant
nor can any person be—yet,
through thick fog of trouble
beauty is her constant friend
not once tainting that which lingers
warm and precious, deep within,

for all the world or universe
cannot match this splendid gift
conjured love 'tween man and woman
surrendered silently, heavenly bliss.

Dawning of a Dream

In each life
>should dawn
>a person
>who is cherished
>dear and true,
>both a lover
>and a friend,
>devotion filled,
>welded truth.

There can be
>no better feeling
>than to have a party—two,
>selfless sharing,
>passions daring,
>as true lovers'
>always caring,
>affection constant,
>solid proof.

Diamonds

Diamonds are unique
true to the cutter
clear and tough
       sparkling
              beautiful
extremely valuable
sentimentally priceless
just like you.

Slavery

Love requiring
the dissolution of dreams,
mulching of spirit,
an obsequious existence,
is not love but slavery.

Bound for Home

She is complex
as truth
yet definable.
Her quests
    swing
              pirouette
      somersault
              lunge
    defy
              exult
    wail
              muse
    rile
              dance
    sulk
              tinkle
    invite
              wink
                    purl.

Paranoid
suspicions
disintegrate.

Resistance staggers
                    trips
                            flops.

Ardor conductor
she guides the train
bound for home.

Heaven and Earth

A girl I saw in passing
her face splashed in mirth,
rolled her eyes toward heaven
so they could fall to earth.

Water Love

Your love is my life spring
a well blossoming
from my heart
rushing through my veins.

Ra

You are my light
the dawn of my days
and the stars of my night.

Garden

There is a garden full and rich
nurtured to maturity by wise hands.
Nourished by soil and sun and rain,
producing a palatable passion fare,
a savory crop for all to feast,
abound in beauty and sustenance.

Silver Needle, Silver Hair

I watched my mother execute
the ancient skill of sewing.

Her swollen fingers
made nimble passes

tugging white thread taut
with a silver needle

through multi-colored cloth.

Each delicate stitch
formed a perfect hump

along her imaginative road
of a pretty pretty blouse

for her unborn grandbaby.

She hummed as she worked
not wired to a digital player,

television an opaque eye,
alone with her craft

and a soft lit lamp.

Her head bowed forward,
her satiny silver hair

radiating a placid shine
seated in a chair

customized by time
to her bulbous body.

Brass Button

She stared quizzically
at the ornate brass button
turned it over in her weathered hands
studied it in the sunlight
watched it twinkle and beam.
Where did she know it?
It whispered to her
like a diamond in black sand.
Twenty years past to the day
it was her mother's button
and her mother's before
stretching back to her native land.
She placed it in her shirt pocket
for safekeeping.

Cradle of Wisdom

Cradled in the steely gray locks
of his father's ancient beard
a giddy baby fidgets.

Across his son's callow brow
       grazes
his seasoned right hand.

The child settles
into his fur soft nest
with a pensive smile.

Parenthood

   At
        the
               fulcrum
                       of
                             our
                                       universe
                               are
                       our
             sons
         and
daughters.

Crests upon mountain crests,
churning at our deepest depths,
molten core of our indigenous souls.

Life Force

One area I lack familiarity is
the cellular structure of living things,
yet I enjoy flights into such blind regions,
unsettling possibilities of what might be
-- like the other day.
Prone in my Strat-O-Lounger,
enjoying a chilled glass of Chablis,
the subject of DNA popped into my head.
Drawing upon my minimal knowledge
of biochemistry,
I recollected DNA is the building block of life.
From there my imagination made
extravagant strains of supposition.
Suppose, I thought, *all physical life*
could be traced to a solitary cell.
A cell composed of self-perpetuating energy.
This energy, through scientific study,
is determined to be thee Life Force.
Further studies reveal that on
instinctual levels all life can
communicate through cells.
With communication lines open
between all living matter
an entire world surfaces.
Through instinct we could sense
the essence of every being,
thereby, create a delicate bond
that cannot be ignored.
Ignorance bows to concrete knowledge
that leads to acceptance
that opens to responsibility
that manifest dependency.
If such a consanguineous link exists;
perhaps it is our physical connection with God.
"Nah!" I said aloud.

"That would be too easy."
About then I poured myself
another glass of wine,
grabbed the TV remote,
and pondered
whether to order Italian or Chinese.

Heaven's Gate

When I think of you
my world floats away
moonlit starry nights
drifting summer days
love has gone astray.

Your heart will not forgive
pain waits by my bed
if only I had listened
to what the dreamer said,
and he said stop!
check the future
open up your life
follow sweet surrender
let the feeling light your life.

What am I to do dear?
when I abandoned you
stampeding all our dreams
beneath my juvenile schemes
young fools have no fear.

Your heart will not forgive
pain waits by my bed
if only I had listened
to what the dreamer said,
and she said stop!
check the future
open up your life
follow sweet surrender
let the feeling light your life.

If I begged and crawled
let shameful tears descend
until past washed away
could you stand to chance?
one fragile moment spent
outside heaven's gates,
and I say stop!
check my soul, love
grieving and ashamed
asking not forgiveness
but a chance of being friends.

Time has robbed me of you
junked on memory's way
seeking new beginnings
nothing left to say.
And they said stop!

Pleasure

Air and I enjoy each other.
It cools my skin
and the heat from my body
excites it to life.

Speak Not

Speak not gingerly
of want
but of desire.

Bashful

There was a woman staring at me
with soft brown eyes,
in an inciting way
that enticingly feminine way
that excites my stomach into somersaults
and pricks my mind to ask, "What if?"

Her smooth peach skin and curvaceous limbs
made me skittish
so I looked away
from her succulent lips and globular hips
because I couldn't stand the heat,
and you know what they say.

Ballads, Lyrics and Melodies (A Love Poem)

When I think of your love
two syllables, soft and gentle
I am like, peace in a groove
living in a daydream
a fantasy real
it fills me up
like words to a melody
harmonizing ecstasy
deep in my soul
ataraxia and blessings manifest
forever is the promise in our hearts
be my refuge and keep me from the storm
slide down into these arms of mine
hold me safe, in honor bound
you can trust that from this moment
before the grace of you, go I
breaking away the clouds surrounding me
my power, my pleasure, my pain
I am part of you indefinitely
wrapped in your warm delicate breeze
reeling me so close to my fantasy
time is the space between me and you
fading into us, two, we
adrift on the murmur of a brook
at eventide.

That's the way love goes.

Her Beauty Makes Me Bashful

I know not what
I see not why
but in her face
of obtuse lines
abides a peace
or semblance to
every aspect
found in you.

Bear with our dream
of love sincere,
promises forged,
on wings of care
delight in happiness
marvelous doubt
ours is pure nectar
that will never sour.

Alone

She slipped seductively
into bed
awakening my manhood
with slow
erotic strokes.

Kissing here
touching there
the fever spread.

Smoldering
sweltering inferno,
passion swooped upon us . . .
then hovered.

Our bodies,
spent
curled into each other
as we cozily drifted off to sleep.

Then the alarm sounded
and I was painfully alone.

While Working

While working, my thoughts turned to romance. A rolling, green, tree laced field, with a cool, blue, running brook permeated the landscape. A brown-eyed woman strolled beside me toward the brook, holding firm my hand. My heart was warmed by her presence. My soul overjoyed by her effervescent glow of life. A dream personified into a female of pleasing shape, beauty, and spirit. As the sun glanced off her golden, delicate skin, she welcomed me into her arms as the morning glory welcomes the sun at dawn. Enticing visions of this lady walking with me caressed every atom of my mind. Wings of desire flew her tender, subtle kisses to my eagerly awaiting lips. Warm breezes blew her bashful hand upward to gently brush my brow. The nectar of honest love that is given and returned is always sweet. A day may turn to night so that it may only turn to day again, that was how my world evolved around her. Unfortunately, love, nor thoughts of such, can pay the bills. So, I promptly got back to work.

Rapture

Yes it is true
my depth of affection
shallows ocean floors
defies gravity's' force
constrains times' hands
alters fates' destiny
weaned, by the lucid embers
of your honeyed abysmal eyes
transcending me deeper
deeper
deepest
into the place of your beginning,
and mine,
intertwined
locked in reverence
suspended in a universe
dimensionless and infinite.

I . . . well,
— you know.

Engaged

Our eyes
touch
engage
focus
hope
hesitate
granting doubt
mounting advantage.

We timidly drift
apart
nursing
liquid courage
needing
concrete signs
what we seek
awaits.

Pleasure

Air and I enjoy each other.
It cools my skin
and the heat from my body
excites it to life.

Us

In my heart
you live
bringing your soul
home to me.

Soul Mate

If the eyes are indeed
the windows to the soul
then how do the blind
discover their soul mates?

Woman

Silken skin
gleaming gold
splendid, tender,
blessed to hold.

Supple gaze
treasured kiss
vibrant, strong,
scintillating bliss.

Frigid like winter
torrid as life
lofty, steadfast,
bold with desire.

Bashful, alluring
nectar and mist
soft scented mixture
Woman is this.

I Don't Wanna Be No Superman

I don't wanna leap tall buildings in a single bound
or deflect hostile bullets with the "S" on my chest,
I don't wanna out race a speeding locomotive
or change into tights in a public phone booth.
(You can be arrested for that you know?)
I don't wanna hear a pin drop from a mile away
or see through buildings or your blouse—
well, maybe enough x-ray vision
to see through your blouse—
for a stolen moment of voyeuristic pleasure—
but aside from that. I don't want it!
I don't wanna be a beacon of strength
shining for every honest sentient being
and feared by eccentric criminal masterminds.
All I want is to be respected or rejected
as a man, a lover, a confidant, a father,
a dreamer who carves out a few selfish cravings
dying with hankering and wonder
still dripping from my lips.

All I *want* is you.

If I am who you desire—
first, second, fifth or tenth
on your long or short checklist of men,
if I fill enough of your chalice
then take of me one curious sip,
a taste, a gargle, a swish or a rinse,
spit out or swallow
the choice is always yours,
from that vintage sampling
should affirmative be your pleasure
vow I you this, to be that modest suit.
tailored from plain thread made of common men,
my only request being to try me on
see if I fit—aside from a prudent tuck or nip,
if so, and I do,
then tantalize me with your opals of tomorrow
for now, your company is all I request
in my car, for I cannot fly,
to my home, earthbound, not in the sky.

Superwomen need not apply.

Elegance

Elegance is a word
encompassed within its syllables
are your eyes
your lips
and your smile,
exclamation mark
on my heart,
italicized in my soul,
as is my love
for who you are
and who you will become.

Probing For Desire

Rain had stopped
sky, a bleary blue.
Parked cars resemble
metal beasts
stilled in time
in a car park lot museum
their large blind eyes
dispassionately gazing at the world.

We make eye contact,
the lovely woman,
with eyes as large as the Mona Lisa,
sitting at the bar
primly eating minestrone soup
as if the world were watching
each steaming spoonful
pass her delicate pink lips.

Maybe she's trying
to glean the attention
of the man wearing
an Armani suit
sitting cross-legged and confident
at the table ahead of me.
(I always sell myself short.
It's easier than being
disappointed again.)

Sunlight battles clouds for recognition.
Wind adds its legions to the fray.
She has nice legs, I think.
I can see them
sheathed in black stockings
her brown leather jacket
falling short
of her black leather mini.

I stare through
a clear glass window.
The blind metal beasts stare back.
Sunlight is victorious.
A woman in a tight blue dress
rushes by.
She smiles.
I turn my head away.

A man joined the woman
in black stockings and mini.
She kisses him with affection.
He sits on a stool beside her.
She turned her back
to face him,
to hear his words,
to conjoin his world.

Her laughter peels desire
from my pining lungs
dribbling its essence
onto my chin,
bringing to mind cardinals
and ice picks
and strobe lit crimson passages
weaving through pulsing caverns.

"What do you know of death?"

the mouth of Don Quixote questioned
a broad shouldered man
with a round, soft middle
gigantic hands
wide feet
spindly legs
and no head.

The man shrugged his shoulders.
The caverns shook.
He stared through plate glass
at an incomprehensible
gray world
pondering peace of mind.
"Been waiting long?"
her companion asked.

True Love Lies

She boasts of love in such honest ways
I cannot resist her nectar
(though watered with chimera)
addressing me as if a virgin lover,
ignorant in manners of such a deed.
I delude myself with her whispers of youth,
words rooted in barren soil,
still I regard this reverent pyrite
as tempered truth, pure as gold.
Whenever is love uttered does she lie?
Whenever do I speak sincerely of age?
The heart's noblest feature
is deflecting harsh candor
and draping subtle peace
over venerable bones.
As well-meaning frauds we so exist,
in our world of liars bliss.

Criminal Passion

A bounty of energy basked in turpitude
is the carnage of defiled lust;
for once it is unleashed,
lust is a treasonous endeavor
crushing long erected pillars
of control and pride and dignity
that measure the worth of civilized man.

So well it is disguised,
a sumptuous flower adorned
with delicate petals of fiery light,
entrancing the fleshy eyes
and enticing the fevered palate
tempting souls—in blind haste
to devour the plant with internal thorns,

Its digestion as painful as sin,
and still, life's most addictive food.
We pursue this insane pleasure-pain
having full knowledge
it incinerates our spirits
in flames of cursed passion;
and yet we feast.

ESP

I want to have a conversation with you
using Extra-Sensory-Perception.
Not for reasons of scientific curiosity
or philosophical debates
or whimsical diatribes or political banter,
but for intimacy, sensuality, lust,
concupiscent, obscene, unabridged sex,
stimulating our carnal appetites
through our supercharged gray cells
like lasers irradiating boundless energy;
an irrepressible force focused behind our eyes
whetted by words becoming salacious images,
for my part, forming such delectable visions as:
the creaminess of your thighs,
the sweet softness of your breast,
the warm succulent nectar dripping
from your silken pink diamond nest,
that erotic smile,
those inviting lips and hips
and ardent eyes that burn and pop
with such sizzle and style
that my erect fire hose makes
a tremulous offer of brave seamen
to quell your furious flames,
and allay your seizures and eruptions,
only to no avail, only to know a veil,
as you writhe and pump and grind and wriggle
yourself into a steamy exhaustion
while I marvel at your shockwaves of pleasure
and your ability to survive
such a torrent physical ordeal.

I want to know what it is
for our minds to make love
with such passion and force
that we are blind to you and me
and know only the merger of us.
I want you to be a part of me in a way
I already know in my heart.

Would it be as good?

Or would it lack that immeasurable spark?

Burn

What is it that you say?
What is it that you do?
How is it that you stroll into a room?
And I ignite.
Am I experiencing a Love Jones?
      Infatuation Jones?
            Erotic Jones?
                  Lust Jones?
                        Jones Jones?

I recollect kissing you from head to toe
front to back
taking my time
around your electric sides,
your searing thighs,
your liquid lips
your fiery hips
your softly closed eyes;
listening with all of my being for that
deep, long, breathy, satisfying sigh
telegraphing me that I had arrived
at the butterfly doorsteps of heaven's gates.

I kept knocking with my hands
until you opened.

I kept knocking with my fingers
until you opened.

I kept knocking with my lips
until you opened.

I kept knocking with my tongue
until you opened.

I kept knocking with my breath,
hot on your neck,
steaming your cheeks, both front and back,
until you opened.

I kept knocking with my soul
until you opened.

I tuned into you
my antennae at the ready
your body, your voice, your movements
your sounds, your breathing, your touches
your kisses, caresses, squeezes,
rubs, throbs, strokes, hugs,
until you opened wide
inviting me inside
for us to continue our sultry pleasure ride.

I wanted you to listen.
Not throttle back your passion but just listen.
Deep in the bowels of our inferno.
    Listen.
Deep in the inferno of our fever.
    Listen.
Would you have heard the same as I?
Was that your heartbeat…or mine?

I Won't, I Will

I won't mention the brilliance you constantly display
at every level of discussion we have encountered, and how
mentally stimulating I find you.

I won't consider your fierce, often unyielding will,
which I respect and resent with equal admiration.

I won't ponder your mischievous, playful manner,
frequently using me as your wanton toy.

I won't tell you of my obvious attempts to deceive
you and have amused you instead.

I won't conjure up images of your supple, sumptuous
body rendering me helpless at a mere glance.

I won't speak of the smooth, aggressive way you cause
my body to quake with titillating pleasure.

I will say, "I love you," and hope that you feel the same…
about me that is.

So Long, Sweetheart

I meant it when I said goodbye
not see you later
have a nice life
it's been real
but *good* & *bye*.

I don't want to see
your smile
or your style
around here anymore.

If you need someone
call someone—*else*
no favors, no chats
no dewy sentiments of longing.

I meant the meanest,
cruelest, bitterest, vilest,
deadliest of farewells
when *I* said *good-bye*;

unless you've changed your mind
      about us?

Missing You

Guarded within an obscure album
photographs of you and I
entwined together
love stamped in our eyes.

Photographs, like memories
forge all remaining links
rekindling wondrous years
of how we came to be.

An osmium heavy burden
supplants a vital heart
and like the spring of youth,
I will always miss you.

Stone Heart

Your love is a black hole
I did not seek;
I did not request, connive, flirt,
romance or desire your heart.
Your emotions are yours to—
command?—control?
or at least—direct?
wrestle?
        unearth?
                focus?
                      suppress?
Not mine to repel
or even reflect
on wanton dire needs
or thwarted attempts to connect.
Whatever deemed authority
you may possess
over fickle amour,
exercise it;
flick that tender spark
at other kindling,
there is no gentle flame
awaiting you here.

Distance

Vast distances
sojourn precariously
a sullen heart,
aloof and skittering
headlong,
down Lover's run,
spilling insanely
amidst gold rich,
romantic fields
of yester-loves.

Estranged

I wanted to get as close as I could.
Pour myself into her
through the pores of her skin.
Become one in the way
uninhibited lovemaking made us.
Incubate so near to her in space and time
that the I in me would become superfluous
with no room for me to exist.

I yearn for living to be as it was.
When love was paramount between us;
no irrational battles over fictitious affairs
money or petty differences;
I need her back in my world.
Back in my home…
back in my bed…
returned to my life.

Writing, My Love

I must write!
It is my blood,
steadily cursing through throbbing veins.
I breathe deep its sultry essence,
taste its sweet and bitter fruit,
drink heartily its soulful essence,
rich in body from fermented youth.
How often I sense its wonder,
growing full beneath my wings,
reaching higher, an endless soaring,
heaven sent, where angels sing.
I grow frightened of its fury,
racing pulse seems so extreme.
Anger rolls with deafening thunder,
spewing forth its rancid name.
Born of need, reared in sorrow,
housed in a void of constant pain.
Never knowing with each tomorrow,
is this orphan to be ashamed?
It is my lover pure and simple,
truest companion, dearest friend.
While at times, it's most distressing,
Always dictating such strict demands.
Writing lay your heavy head
upon my hardened, muscled breast,
In my arms, you'll find warm comfort,
close your eyes and simply rest.
If no other ever loves you,
you will always find in me,
one who ask not many questions,
love unfaltering, blind and true.

Absence of Desire

An emotion? a craving? a yearning? a ravenous hunger?
for that *some*-one or *some*-thing
wading amongst teeming waters of longing
plunging headlong, heartfelt into motivation
suffocating in a diaphanous sea
screaming into the gray sponge of apathy
hearing oneself, here in one's self
contemplating if the passion of WANT still lives.

Toxic purple fire capriciously belches
willful hopes, lush dreams, reckless aspirations
into blind white caverns of nothingness
never quenching an insatiable carcass
harboring a sieve for a gut,
emptiness digesting vacancy
spawning nutrition and substance
for the body of terminal abyss.

Paradise

This morning, I strolled to the shore
to watch the sunrise.
Dewy blue sky kissed a gentle emerald ocean
on a limpid horizon.
A bright red ball sat suspended
in the distance upon an invisible thread.
Seagulls glided near the edge of the world
echoing sentiments from God that all is well.
Cool copper sand formed grainy sandals
beneath my bare, chilly feet.
Water caressed the shore for a lover's moment
before returning home.
Damp salt breezes tingled my skin;
all sounds seduced my mind.
        Paradise.
                And through it all,
                      I longed for you.

Infinite Loves

If there are incalculable molecules
within a finite galaxy,
can there be
infinite loves
within one life,
one heart,
one soul?

Lonely Heart

Oh lonely heart, you're tired and worn
the clothes you're wearing are old and torn
with each grudging step you move ahead
in the prospect that love will arise.

Faith is the only food you eat.
Tears are the only water you drink.

If hope were garments, you'd be dressed like a king.
If suffering were gold, you'd own everything.
If dreams were a blanket, you'd forever be warm.
If patience were light, you'd outshine the sun.

You look at yourself, standing there,
beaten and restless and full of despair,
asking yourself the question, why?
As always, the answer is silence of mind.

Oh lonely heart, do not be forlorn
for at your expedition's end

Will arise a glowing, compassionate heart
bringing with it peace of exonerate fortitude,
joy of extraordinary magnitude,
and abysmal love as honest as truth.

Once your pilgrimage has united you with
that kindred heart of destiny,
then lonely heart,
your solitude will cease to exist.

Self Sacrifice

When winds cease
and liquid tear-shaped prisms fall
saturating our springy woolen curls,
tracing our skin slick limbs,
purging our individualism
—will you come?

Will you faithfully relinquish,
without fear,
minus misgivings,
your threadbare soul
to the uncertain promise
        of us?

Henna Eyes

Embraced by the warmth of *Ye Olde Bagel Shoppe*
"May I help you?" she asks,
from behind a glass display fortress
of bagels, pastries, cream cheese and lox,
her henna eyes are vulnerable this morning,
her liberal russet hair restrained in a bun
by a carnivorous comb that bit
but never chewed;
her long silken eyelashes —
lighter than helium —
teased, with her fawning smile,
a silver stud attached to her tongue
announced itself every syllable she spoke;
she moves as only women are privileged
at ease in innate feminine ways,
the smell of roasted coffee brewing
tickles, recycling childhood memories
of breakfast at home,
too young to sip coffee then,
old enough for tea
and chocolate
and sodas
and shoestring licorice.

Too young for vulnerable henna eyes.

Human Contact

We have touched one another
as light touches images to eyes,
    a flash,
a frame of recognition,
    processed by brain cells
against previous experiences
    and original thoughts.

Unexpected Rendezvous

I was slapped in the face by a memory tonight:
in a tavern, bright and cheerful,
with a sober state of mind.

Her appearance stifled gorgeous
to say the absolute least,
sprinkled gingerly with honey dew
from her head to her feet.
While I must confess
she came as a shock,
my mind diligently struggled
in a foolish attempt to block.
Eager eyes roamed about
seeking a solitary face,
which at least for the moment
could take the ghost lady's place.
Idiotic was my quest
for like a child firmly scorned,
"Don't touch that, you'll get burned!"
I quickly shrugged loose the warning.
A cool, tranquil desire
floated my eyes in her direction,
upon a bar stool she sat
in all her feminine perfection.
Skin lithe, glowing, sweet shade of gold,
hair, black, curly, midnight stars to behold.
Eyes, brown and lucid, soft as a rose,
with a minted smile beneath an inverted club nose.

And oh my God, what a smile that woman has!

Teeth made of pearls, darned especially for her,
lips full and sensual, with a half moon curve,
pert girlish dimples, embedded in smooth supple cheeks,
alluring, fixating, how could such a woman be?
Suddenly I felt imprisoned
I stood reeling within her cell,
when from her silken throat
streamed firm seductive sounds
stalking feverously, I thought,
"Let me out! Let me out!"
"Fool," echoed the voice of reason,
"You are lost, can you not sense."
"take a deep, uncensored breath,"
"Smell her unique hypnotic scent"
"that's not some accidental fragrance,"
"it's an aphrodisiac mint."
"Erupting times of precious moments,"
"Escaped you two in innocent bliss."

I was slapped in the face by a memory tonight:
quietly slipping in and out,
the front door of my life.

Infatuation

Her lips varied in motion,
apparently in speech,
curling at ends
displaying alabaster teeth,
while I listened
intrigued,
as a child engulfed in imaginative
telling of ancient Indian legends
around a midnight campfire.
Her words eluded my ears.
Still I listened.
Her smile sparkled
in the cold, blue night,
sedating fixed brown eyes
like warm milk,
soothing my jittery tummy.

Potpourri, Kiss Me and Soul

Mellifluous flutters of delicate fragrances
flitting its scents upon unbridled senses,
beyond smell, before passion,
bubbling within the warm belly of desire —
not lust, for that is turbulent desire
existing on another plane —
but a longing for touch
and tender, enduring gazes.

The tongue is still
when the soul is talking,
a wondrous enigma of our imperfection,
for during times when our hearts are full
silence is how it is best expressed,
and when the lips noblest function
are to pucker themselves for a kiss.

To experience such pleasure,
to excite such a flame,
is when heaven on earth
and earth in heaven
are one in the same.

Longings

Out there,
    somewhere,
she waits,
    dissecting her life,
as I,
    pondering
who?
    when?
        how?
            if?
our destiny will happen.

Scripture

She asked me to explain why I love her.

I began my foolish answer quest
in the harbor of her pristine eyes,
moved to her beautiful face,
arrived at her stinging wit,
skipped to her sensuous body,
banked at her fiery temper,
tripped on her sultry tongue,
climbed along her motherland hair,
staggered through her brilliant mind,
hiked into her benevolent heart,
lapped at her natural spring,
settling in her tender soul.

Brightly wrapped honorable clichés
bearing sincere gifts
from my sandpaper lips,
attempting to bring into vivid focus
that which places her first in my affection,
not a solitary word articulated or muttered
at a crystal moment of ardent truth --
all be they summary facts! --
of her who I love.
Had I voiced what I profess
as bone marrow, unequivocal faith,
to my true Love's resounding "Why?"
In blunt, bold-face, honest honesty
I love you *because*
I love YOU.

This much I know...

The simple scripture of my soul.

Harmony and Grace

In sweet revelry of times
orchestrating their windsongs
upon an effervescent bubble
of scent and melody,
come forth all climes
to create a world
so peaceful and spacious and caring
of all— not one—
not the chosen—
not the few—
but every *who* they encounter,
brave spirit of life,
warrior soul of love.

Love Eternal

Love does not perish with the flesh
it is as everlasting as a lazy summer's day
whistling through our wholesome memory
like wind within a forest green
racing through our eclipsing youth
evaporating from view in time
as a bright face in graying mist
radiating from our solar core
hibernating in warm crystal sands
where we slumber nude
beneath a dazzling shelter of stars
harbored within our humanity cradle
cemented there for all time.

Notes

<u>Song quotes for *Ballads, Lyrics and Melodies (A Love Poem)*</u>

"When I think of your love"—Brownstone, "5 Miles to Empty"

"And a word that's soft and gentle"—Al Jarreau, "Try A Little Tenderness."

"I was like, peace in a groove"—TLC, "Diggin' on You."

"I'm living in a kind of daydream"—Natalie Cole, "The Very Thought of You."

"A fantasy real"—Maxwell, "Ascension (Don't Ever Wonder)."

"It fills me up"—Luther Vandross, Gregory Hines duet), "There's Nothing Better than Love."

"Like words to a melody"—Natalie Cole, "Inseparable."

"Harmonizing ecstasy"—Quincy Jones, "The Secret Garden."

"Deep in my heart"—Babyface, "Love Makes Things Happen."

"Peace and blessings manifest"—Erykah Badu, "On & On."

"Forever is the promise in our hearts"—Brian McKnight, "Anytime."

"Baby be my refuge and keep me from the storm"—Oleta Adams, "Hold Me for A While."

"Slide down into these arms of mine"—Oleta Adams, "Get Here."

"Hold me safe, in honor bound"—Vanessa Williams, "Higher Ground."

"You can know that from this moment"—Tevin Campbell, "Always in My Heart."

"Before the grace of you, go I"—Simon and Garfunkel, "Kathy's Song."

"Breaks away the clouds surrounding me"—Mariah Carey, "Music Box."

"My power, my pleasure, my pain"—Seal, "Kiss from a Rose."

"I am part of you indefinitely"—Mariah Carey, "Always Be My Baby."

"Wrapped in your warm gentle breeze"—Mariah Carey, "Underneath the Stars."

"You've got me so close to my dreams"—En Vogue, "Hooked on Your Love."

"Time is the space between me and you"—Seal, "Prayer for the Dying."

You were fading into me"—Mariah Carey, "Always Be My Baby."

"The murmur of a brook"—Natalie Cole, "Stella by Starlight."

"At eventide"—Natalie Cole, "Stella by Starlight."

"That's the way love goes"—Janet Jackson, "Design of a Decade."

Acknowledgements

Acknowledgement and thanks to the editors and staff of the following publications in which versions of these poems first appeared:

Ashes to Ashes, Poetry Press: "Whirlpool"

Golden Apple Press: "DNA," "Still We Laugh" and "Infatuation"

Loose Gravel: "The Screen"

The Armadillo Poetry Press: "Infinite Loves" and "Paradise"

The Aurorean: "Human Contact"

The Raintown Review: "Natural Evolution"

Sandbox (Bare Bones Press): "Human Contact," "Infatuation", "Infinite Loves," "Longings," "Paradise," "Scripture," "Self Sacrifice," and "The I Factor"

A Drop of Midnight (Bare Bones Press): "Bound for Home," "Harmony and Grace," "Henna Eyes," "I Don't Wanna Be No Superman," "Parenthood," "Potpourri, Kiss Me and Soul," and "Stone Heart"

Michael R Lane was born and raised in Pittsburgh, Pennsylvania. Michael studied English Literature and Creative Writing at Point Park University, Sonoma State University, and Portland State University. He has written poetry for more than three decades, and has had poetry published in numerous journals.

www.ingramcontent.com/pod-product-compliance
Lightning Source LLC
Chambersburg PA
CBHW032041290426
44110CB00012B/905